DISCARD

TO SEE THE
WORLD AFRESH

TO SEE
THE WORLD
AFRESH

Compiled by
Lilian Moore and Judith Thurman

Atheneum 1974 *New York*

In memory of Pablo Neruda

Copyright © 1974 by Lilian Moore and Judith Thurman
All rights reserved
Library of Congress catalog card number 73–84831
ISBN *0–689–30141–3*
Published simultaneously in Canada by
McClelland & Stewart, Ltd.
Manufactured in the United States of America
by Halliday Lithograph Corporation
West Hanover, Massachusetts
Designed by Nancy Gruber
First Edition

'74997'

Centralia Junior High School
Centralia, Washington

Acknowledgments

We gratefully acknowledge the following permissions:

A. R. Ammons. "After Yesterday," and "Saying," from *Briefings, Poems Small and Easy*, W. W. Norton & Co., Inc. Copyright © 1971 by A. R. Ammons and reprinted by permission of the publisher.

Miguel Angel Asturias. "The Indians Come Down from Mixco," translated by Donald Devenish Walsh, from *An Anthology of Latin American Poetry*, edited by Dudley Fitts. Copyright 1942 by New Directions Publishing Corporation. Reprinted by permission of New Directions Publishing Corporation.

Margaret Atwood. "Carrying Food Home in Winter," from *Procedures for Underground*. Copyright © 1969 by Modern Poetry Association. Reprinted by permission of Little, Brown and Co. in association with The Atlantic Monthly Press.

Robert Bly. "Driving to Town Late to Mail a Letter," from *Silence in the Snowy Fields*, Wesleyan University Press, 1963. Copyright © 1963 by Robert Bly. Reprinted by permission of the author. "Counting the Small-Boned Bodies," and "Looking into a Face," from *The Light Around the Body*, Harper & Row. Copyright © 1967 by Robert Bly. Reprinted by permission of Harper & Row, Publishers, Inc.

Edwin Brock. "Five Ways to Kill a Man," from *Invisibility Is the Art of Survival*. Copyright © 1972 by Edwin Brock. Reprinted by permission of New Directions Publishing Corp.; and from *Penguin Modern Poets 8*, Reprinted by permission of David Higham Associates, Ltd.

Joseph Bruchac. "The Drum-Maker," from *Indian Mountain and Other Poems*, Ithaca House. Reprinted by permission of the publisher.

Michael Casey. "A Bummer," from *Obscenities*. Copyright © 1972 by Yale University. Reprinted by permission of Yale University Press.

Lucille Clifton. "the discoveries of fire," "in the inner city," "The 1st," from *Good Times*. Copyright © 1969 by Lucille Clifton. Reprinted by permission of Random House, Inc.

Malcolm Cowley. "Still Life," and "A Smoke of Birds," from *Blue Juniata: Collected Poems*. Copyright © 1967, 1968 by Malcolm Cowley. Reprinted by permission of The Viking Press, Inc.

James Dickey. "Bums, on Waking," "Deer Among Cattle." Copyright © 1963, 1965 by James Dickey, from *Poems 1957–1967*. Reprinted by permission of Wesleyan University Press. "Bums, on Waking" first appeared in *The New Yorker*.

Robert Frost. "Dust of Snow," and "Nothing Gold Can Stay," from *The Poetry of Robert Frost*, edited by Edward Connery Latham. Copyright 1923 © 1969 by Holt, Rinehart and Winston, Inc. Copyright 1951 by Robert Frost. Reprinted by permission of Holt, Rinehart and Winston, Inc.

Paul Goodman. "Kent State,' May 4, 1970," from *Homespun of Oatmeal Gray*. Copyright © 1969, 1970 by Paul Goodman. Reprinted by permission of Random House, Inc.

Jonathan Griffin. "Storm End." Reprinted by permission of the author.

Langston Hughes. "The Negro Speaks of Rivers." Copyright 1926 by Alfred A. Knopf, Inc. and renewed 1954 by Langston Hughes. From *Selected Poems*. Reprinted by permission of the publisher.

Ted Hughes. "Bullfrog," from *Lupercal*. Copyright © 1959 by Ted Hughes. Originally appeared in *The New Yorker*. Reprinted by permission of Harper & Row, Publishers, Inc., and by permission of Faber & Faber Ltd., London.

Randall Jarrell. "The Bird of Night," and "Bats," from *The Bat-Poet*. Copyright © Macmillan Publishing Company, Inc., 1963, 1964. Reprinted by permission of Macmillan Publishing Co., Inc.

Leroi Jones (Imamu Amiri Baraka). "Young Soul," from *Black Magic Poetry 1961–1967*. Copyright © 1969 by Leroi Jones, Reprinted by permission of the publisher, The Bobbs-Merrill Company, Inc.

June Jordan. "Maybe the Birds," from *Some Changes*. Copyright © 1967, 1971 by June Meyer Jordan. Published by E. P. Dutton & Co., Inc. and reprinted by their permission.

Kamimura Hajime. "Firefly," from *Post-War Japanese Poetry*, edited and translated by Harry and Lynn Guest and Kajima Shozo. Copyright © Kamimura Hajime 1972. Translation copyright © Harry Guest, Lynn Guest, Kajima Shozo, 1972. Reprinted by permission of the author and of Penguin Books, Ltd.

Maxine Kumin. "The Presence," from *The Nightmare Factory*. Copyright © 1970 by Maxime Kumin. Reprinted by permission of Harper & Row, Publishers, Inc.

Philip Larkin. "First Sight," from *Whitsun Weddings*. Faber & Faber, Ltd. Reprinted by permission of Faber & Faber, Ltd., London.

Denise Levertov. "The Coming Fall," from *O Taste and See*. Copyright © 1964 by Denise Levertov Goodman. Reprinted by permission of New Directions Publishing Corporation.

George Macbeth. Part 1 of "A Riddle," from *The Night of Stones*. Copyright © 1968 by George Macbeth. Reprinted by permission of Atheneum Publishers, and by permission of Macmillan, London and Basingstoke.

W. S. Merwin. "Fog-Horn," Copyright © 1958 by W. S. Merwin. First appeared in *The New Yorker*. Reprinted by permission of Harold Ober Associates, Inc. "For a Coming Extinction," from *The Lice*. Copyright © 1967 by W. S. Merwin. First appeared in *The Southern Review*. Reprinted by permission of Atheneum Publishers.

Robert Mezey. "There," from *The Door Standing Open*, Houghton Mifflin Company. Reprinted by permission of the author, and from *The Door Standing Open*. Copyright © 1970 Oxford University Press. Reprinted by permission of the publisher.

Marianne Moore. "Poetry," from *Collected Poems*, Copyright 1935 by Marianne Moore, renewed 1963 by Marianne Moore and T. S. Eliot. Reprinted with the permission of Macmillan Publishing Company, Inc.

Charles Olsen, "These Days," from *Archeologist of Morning*. All rights reserved. Reprinted by permission of Grossman Publishers.

Nicanor Parra. First five stanzas of "Manifesto," from *Emergency Poems*, translated by Miller Williams. Copyright © 1962 by Nicanor Parra and Miller Williams. Reprinted by permission of New Directions Publishing Corporation.

Octavio Paz. "Dawn," from *New Poetry of Mexico*, edited by Mark Strand. Copyright © 1966 by Siglo XXI Editores, S. A. English translation © 1970 by E. P. Dutton and Co., Inc., publishers, and reprinted by their permission.

Fernando Pessoa (Alberto Caiero). "XIV—I don't bother with rhymes," translated by Jonathan Griffin, from *Alberto Caiero*, Volume 1 of *The Selected Poems of Fernando Pessoa*. Carcanet Press, Cheadle, Cheshire. Reprinted by permission of the publisher.

Marge Piercy. "Simple Song," from *Hard Loving*. Copyright © 1969 by Marge Piercy. Reprinted by permission of Wesleyan University Press; "Councils," copyright © 1971 by Marge Piercy. Reprinted by permission of Doubleday & Company, Inc.

Sylvia Plath. "For a Fatherless Son," from *Winter Trees*. Copyright © 1971 by Ted Hughes. First appeared in *The New Yorker*. Reprinted by permission of Harper & Row, Publishers, Inc., and by Faber & Faber, Ltd., London.

Vasco Popa, "Donkey," from *Selected Poems*, translated by Anne Pennington, Penguin Books, Ltd. Reprinted by permission of Olwyn Hughes.

Kenneth Rexroth. "Inversely, as the Square of their Distances Apart," from *Collected Shorter Poems*. Copyright 1944 by New Directions Publishing Corporation. Reprinted by permission of New Directions Publishing Corp.

Yannis Ritsos. "Motionless Swaying," and "After the Rain," from *Gestures and Other Poems*, translated by Nikos Stangos. Reprinted by permission of Jonathan Cape, Ltd., publishers.

Theodore Roethke. "The Meadow Mouse," from *Collected Poems* of *Theodore Roethke*. Copyright © 1963 by Beatrice Roethke, Administratrix of the Estate of Theodore Roethke. Reprinted by permission of Doubleday & Company, Inc.

William Stafford. "Traveling through the Dark," from *Traveling Through the Dark*. Copyright © 1960 by William Stafford. Reprinted by permission of Harper & Row, Publishers, Inc. "Listening," from *The Rescued Year*. Copyright © 1960 by William Stafford, Reprinted by permission of Harper & Row, Publishers, Inc.

Wallace Stevens. "Thirteen Ways of Looking at a Blackbird," from *The Collected Poems of Wallace Stevens*. Copyright 1923 and renewed 1951 by Wallace Stevens. Reprinted by permission of Alfred A. Knopf, Inc.

Adrien Stoutenberg. "Sky Diver," and "Is Is Like Is," from *Short History of The Fur Trade*, Houghton Mifflin Company. Reprinted by permission of the publisher. "Affinities," from *Heroes, Advise Us*. Copyright © 1964 by Adrien Stoutenberg. Reprinted by permission of Curtis Brown, Ltd.

Brian Swann. "Three Riddles," reprinted by permission of the author.

Ryuichi Tamura. "Invisible Tree," from *Japanese Poetry Now*, translated by Thomas Fitzsimmons. Reprinted by permission of André Deutsch, Ltd.

Tewa Indians. "Song of the Sky Loom," from *Songs of The Tewa*, translated by Herbert J. Spinden. Reprinted by permission of Ailes Spinden.

John Updike. "Hoeing," Copyright © 1963 by John Updike. from *Telephone Poles and Other Poems*, first appeared in *The New Yorker*. Reprinted by permission of Alfred A. Knopf, Inc. "Wash," Copyright © 1960 by John Updike, from *Telephone Poles and Other Poems*, First appeared in *The New Yorker*. Reprinted by permission of Alfred A. Knopf, Inc.

David Wagoner. "Staying Alive," and "Words," from *Staying Alive*, Indiana University Press. Reprinted by permission of the publisher.

Ruth Whitman. "Ripeness," from *The Marriage Wig*. Copyright © 1968 by Ruth Whitman. Reprinted by permission of Harcourt Brace Jovanovich, Inc.

William Carlos Williams, "The Term," and "The Red Wheelbarrow from *Collected Earlier Poems*. Copyright 1938 by New Directions Publishing Corporation. Reprinted by permission of New Directions Publishing Corp.

Ryojiro Yamanaka. "Wind," from *Post-War Japanese Poetry*, Penguin Books, Ltd. Reprinted by permission of the author.

Contents

Introduction

In the last section of this book, *A Place for the Genuine,* there is a poem by Marianne Moore that is called "Poetry." The lifetime of Marianne Moore, who was born in 1887 and died in 1972, embraced practically the whole course of what we call "modern" poetry. She and her friends broke with the traditions of the 19th century and wrote in a new way. They went back to the "raw material of poetry in all its rawness"— that is, the objects, the faces, the feelings that they found around them. They rejected the notion of something being inherently "unpoetic." Anything that was "genuine" was now important.

They made another change, too. They listened around until they found a voice—or voices—which were as genuine as those useful objects and ordinary feelings they had begun to write about. These poets no longer spoke in the mythological and romantic language of the 19th century, but like contemporary men and women. "Never write any line," said Ezra Pound, "that you couldn't under *some* circumstances, actually speak."

It is more urgent today, in a world polluted by the synthetic, to find a place for the genuine. It is harder than it was in 1900, when Marianne Moore began to write, to see the world afresh—to make contact with whatever is authentic. We are distracted by city life, television, travel, the news itself. They have overexposed us to the visible and sensible world but they have also kept us remote from it. It is easy to become numb.

Poets restore the flow of sensation. They reach us at that level of our beings "to which we rarely penetrate." They charge us, they move us, they startle us with what we already know, but what we often ignore. For this we should be grateful.

The poems in this collection are organized into seven sections, but they make a circle rather than discrete segments. Insights overlap. *Use the muscle in your heart,* says one poet. *Leave the roots on,* says another, reminding us of what is most perishable—the intensity of the present moment.

Poets have always helped us to see afresh "how fanatic roots are . . . *how deep the earth can be."* But if there is special tension now in our response to the physical world it is because we can't take any part of it for granted anymore.

This awareness seems especially acute when the poets write about animals—*all things innocent*—the cat who "stores its shadow in the black loft of his bones" or a bullfrog who "pumps out whole fogs full of horn." The need to praise the uniqueness of each creature is part of the fear that the "coming extinction" is never far: we are vulnerable like the gray whale "we are sending to the End."

But what the poet sees afresh may sometimes be more elusive than this. Some poems have the quality of riddles. The Greek poet Ritsos asks, *"Is that how it is with poetry?"* Is it unpredictable, elusive? Is its meaning sometimes beyond us? In this section there are poems with answers—riddles—and poems with no answers, whose metaphors can be unriddled, too. To do this, one must ransack one's experience. The reward with the poems, as with the riddles, is recognition.

This recognition is immediate for the poems in *A Human Face.* These are the faces that we know. These are our predicaments. Here one of the poets suggests, ironically, that of five ways to kill a man, the best one may be to leave him in the 20th century. Another protests that to survive "we must sit down and reason together."

These poems are inevitably the center of this collection.

Kerhonkson, N.Y. 　　　　　　　　　　　　LILIAN MOORE,
October 1973. 　　　　　　　　　　　　JUDITH THURMAN

Poetry . . . may help to break up the conventional modes of perception . . . which are perpetually forming, and make people see the world afresh, or some new part of it. It may make us from time to time a little more aware of the deeper, unnamed feelings which form the substratum of our being, to which we rarely penetrate; for our lives are mostly a constant evasion of ourselves, and an evasion of the visible and sensible world.

T. S. Eliot

PART ONE

The Muscle in Your Heart

Young Soul

First, feel, then feel, then
read, or read, then feel, then
fall, or stand, where you
already are. Think
of your self, and the other
selves . . . think
of your parents, your mothers
and sisters, your bentslick
father, then feel, or
fall, on your knees
if nothing else will move you,

then read
and look deeply
into all matters
come close to you
city boys—
country men

Make some muscle
in your head, but
use the muscle
in yr heart

Imamu Amiri Baraka
(Leroi Jones)

Simple Song

When we are going toward someone we say
You are just like me
your thoughts are my brothers
word matches word
how easy to be together.

When we are leaving someone we say
how strange you are
we cannot communicate
we can never agree
how hard, hard and weary to be together.

We are not different nor alike
but each strange in his leather body
sealed in skin and reaching out clumsy hands
and loving is an act
that cannot outlive
the open hand
the open eye
the door in the chest standing open.

Marge Piercy

There

It is deep summer. Far out
at sea, the young squalls darken
and roll, plunging northward,
threatening everything. I see
the Atlantic moving in slow
contemplative fury
against the rocks, the beaten
headlands, and the towns sunk deep
in a blind northern light. Here,
far inland, in the mountains
of Mexico, it is raining
hard, battering the soft mouths
of flowers. I am sullen, dumb,
ungovernable. I taste myself
and I taste those winds, uprisings
of salt and ice, of great trees
brought down, of houses and cries
lost in the storm; and what breaks
on that black shore breaks in me.

Robert Mezey

The 1st

What I remember about that day
is boxes stacked across the walk
and couch springs curling through the air
and drawers and tables balanced on the curb
and us, hollering,
leaping up and around
happy to have a playground;

nothing about the emptied rooms
nothing about the emptied family

Lucille Clifton

1

in the inner city
or
like we call it
home
we think a lot about uptown
and the silent nights
and the houses straight as
dead men
and the pastel lights
and we hang on to our no place
happy to be alive
and in the inner city
or
like we call it
home

Lucille Clifton

Carrying Food Home in Winter

I walk uphill through the snow
hard going
brown paper bag of groceries
balanced low on my stomach,
heavy, my arms stretching
to hold it turn all tendon.

Do we need this paper bag
my love, do we need this bulk
of peels and cores, do we need
these bottles, these roots
and bits of cardboard
to keep us floating
as on a raft
above the snow I sink through?

The skin creates
islands of warmth
in winter, in summer
islands of coolness.

The mouth performs
a similar deception.

I say I will transform
this egg into a muscle
this bottle into an act of love

This onion will become a motion
this grapefruit
will become a thought.

Margaret Atwood

Staying Alive

Staying alive in the woods is a matter of calming down
At first and deciding whether to wait for rescue,
Trusting to others,
Or simply to start walking and walking in one direction
Till you come out—or something happens to stop you.
By far the safer choice
Is to settle down where you are, and try to make a living
Off the land, camping near water, away from shadows.
Eat no white berries;
Spit out all bitterness. Shooting at anything
Means hiking further and further every day
To hunt survivors;
It may be best to learn what you have to learn without a gun,
Not killing but watching birds and animals go
In and out of shelter
At will. Following their example, build for a whole season;
Facing across the wind in your lean-to,
You may feel wilder,
But nothing, not even you, will have to stay in hiding.
If you have no matches, a stick and a fire-bow
Will keep you warmer,
Or the crystal of your watch, filled with water, held up to
    the sun
Will do the same in time. In case of snow
Drifting toward winter,
Don't try to stay awake through the night, afraid of freezing—
The bottom of your mind knows all about zero;
It will turn you over
And shake you till you waken. If you have trouble sleeping
Even in the best of weather, jumping to follow
With eyes strained to their corners
The unidentifiable noises of the night and feeling

Bears and packs of wolves nuzzling your elbow,
Remember the trappers
Who treated them indifferently and were left alone.
If you hurt yourself, no one will comfort you
Or take your temperature,
So stumbling, wading, and climbing are as dangerous as flying.
But if you decide, at last, you must break through
In spite of all danger,
Think of yourself by time and not by distance, counting
Wherever you're going by how long it takes you;
No other measure
Will bring you safe to nightfall. Follow no streams: they run
Under the ground or fall into wilder country.
Remember the stars
And moss when your mind runs into circles. If it should rain
Or the fog should roll the horizon in around you,
Hold still for hours
Or days if you must, or weeks, for seeing is believing
In the wilderness. And if you find a pathway,
Wheel-rut, or fence-wire,
Retrace it left or right: someone knew where he was going
Once upon a time, and you can follow
Hopefully, somewhere,
Just in case. There may even come, on some uncanny evening,
A time when you're warm and dry, well fed, not thirsty,
Uninjured, without fear,
When nothing, either good or bad, is happening.
This is called staying alive. It's temporary.
What occurs after
Is doubtful. You must always be ready for something to come
    bursting
Through the far edge of a clearing, running toward you,
Grinning from ear to ear

And hoarse with welcome. Or something crossing and
    hovering
Overhead, as light as air, like a break in the sky,
Wondering what you are.
Here you are face to face with the problem of recognition.
Having no time to make smoke, too much to say,
You should have a mirror
With a tiny hole in the back for better aiming, for reflecting
Whatever disaster you can think of, to show
The way you suffer.
These body signals have universal meaning: If you are lying
Flat on your back with arms outstretched behind you,
You say you require
Emergency treatment; if you are standing erect and holding
Arms horizontal, you mean you are not ready;
If you hold them over
Your head, you want to be picked up. Three of anything
Is a sign of distress. Afterward, if you see
No ropes, no ladders,
No maps or messages falling, no searchlights or trails blazing,
Then, chances are, you should be prepared to burrow
Deep for a deep winter.

David Wagoner

Looking into a Face

Conversation brings us so close! Opening
The surfs of the body,
Bringing fish up near the sun,
And stiffening the backbones of the sea!

I have wandered in a face, for hours,
Passing through dark fires.
I have risen to a body
Not yet born,
Existing like a light around the body,
Through which the body moves like a sliding moon.

Robert Bly

PART TWO

How Deep the Earth
Can Be

Sky Diver

Grotesque, jumping out
like a clothed frog, helmet and glasses,
arms and legs wading the sky,
feet flapping before the cloth flower opens;
then suspended, poised,
an exclamation point upside-down,
and going down, swaying over corn and creeks
and highways scribbled
over the bones of fish and eagles.

There is the interim between air and earth,
time to study steeples
and the underwings of birds going over,
before the unseen chasm,
the sudden jaw open and hissing.

Lying here after the last jump
I see how fanatic roots are,
how moles breathe through darkness,
how deep the earth can be.

Adrien Stoutenberg

14

from The Coming Fall

Down by the fallen fruit in the old orchard
the air grows cold. The hill
hides the sun.

A sense of the present
rises out of earth and grass,
enters the feet, ascends

into the genitals, constricting
the breast, lightening
the head—a wisdom,

a shiver, a delight
that what is passing

is here, as if
a snake went by, green in the
gray leaves.

Denise Levertov

Song of the Sky Loom

Oh our Mother the Earth oh our Father the Sky
Your children are we
    with tired backs we bring you the gifts you love

So weave for us a garment of brightness

May the warp be the white light of morning
May the weft be the red light of evening
May the fringes be the falling rain
May the border be the standing rainbow

Weave for us this bright garment
that we may walk where birds sing
    where grass is green

Oh our Mother the Earth oh our Father the Sky

Tewa Indians

TRANSLATED BY HERBERT J. SPINDEN

Hoeing

I sometimes fear the younger generation will be deprived
  of the pleasures of hoeing;
  there is no knowing
how many souls have been formed by this simple exercise.

The dry earth like a great scab breaks, revealing
  moist-dark loam—
  the pea-root's home,
a fertile wound perpetually healing.

How neatly the green weeds go under!
  The blade chops the earth new.
  Ignorant the wise boy who
has never performed this simple, stupid, and useful wonder.

John Updike

A Smoke of Birds

Starlings descend at nightfall, wheeling and swarming round
    a bamboo copse or a cedar of Lebanon.

They cross the face of the winter sun like smoke.

A smoke of descending starlings: it takes the form succes-
    sively of a ball, a hoop, a mandolin (or maybe a gui-
    tar), a string of frankfurters, a candy poke

that swells to a balloon and then collapses with a hiss of
    escaping gases.

Out of an emptiness is heard the chittering of birds.

Malcolm Cowley

After the Rain

After the rain, the chirping of the birds sounds more
    emphatic,
scattered, lonely. Mountains have suddenly grown taller,
clouds too. Wet colours are bigger
on the house walls—rose, pistachio, pale blue,
the red canopy of the tavern, drops on the trees
each dropping in a different rhythm, different time, like
    old clocks,
big wooden clocks opened up for repair,
their mechanisms exposed—cogs and more cogs,
small gears, related movements, springs, sounds—
all uncoordinated, left to a blind fate;—what word, I wonder,
would set these broken down clocks with their tormented
    entrails
in the right motion in perfect circles?

Yannis Ritsos

TRANSLATED BY NIKOS STANGOS

Invisible Tree

On the snow I found prints
and for the first time knew
the world of small life,
birds, beasts in the forest:
squirrel, footprints down an old elm,
across the path . . . gone among firs—
no anxiety, hesitation, nowhere
a question:
a fox, coursing straight down the road
through the valley north of my village—
my hunger never drew so straight a line,
never in my mind so smooth, blind, sure
a rhythm:
a bird now, prints clearer than her voice,
claw-marks sharper than her life,
feather-flicks frozen in the sloping snow—
my terror could never tremble to such pattern,
in my mind never such a pagan, sensual,
affirmative beat.

Suddenly—sunset
big on the summit of Asama.
Something now known has built a forest,
pushed open the mouth of the valley,
split the cold air.
Back in my hut
I light the stove
thinking an invisible tree
invisible bird
invisible small things living
rhythm invisible.

Ryuichi Tamura
TRANSLATED BY THOMAS FITZSIMMONS

Dust of Snow

The way a crow
Shook down on me
The dust of snow
From a hemlock tree

Has given my heart
A change of mood
And saved some part
Of a day I had rued.

Robert Frost

Fog-Horn

Surely that moan is not the thing
That men thought they were making, when they
Put it there, for their own necessities.
That throat does not call to anything human
But to something men had forgotten,
That stirs under fog. Who wounded that beast
Incurably, or from whose pasture
Was it lost, full grown, and time closed round it
With no way back? Who tethered its tongue
So that its voice could never come
To speak out in the light of clear day,
But only when the shifting blindness
Descends and is acknowledged among us,
As though from under a floor it is heard,
Or as though from behind a wall, always
Nearer than we had remembered? If it
Was we that gave tongue to this cry
What does it bespeak in us, repeating
And repeating, insisting on something
That we never meant? We only put it there
To give warning of something we dare not
Ignore, lest we should come upon it
Too suddenly, recognize it too late,
As our cries were swallowed up and all hands lost.

W. S. Merwin

Inversely, as the Square of of Their Distances Apart

It is impossible to see anything
In this dark; but I know this is me, Rexroth,
Plunging through the night on a chilling planet.
It is warm and busy in this vegetable
Darkness where invisible deer feed quietly.
The sky is warm and heavy, even the trees
Over my head cannot be distinguished,
But I know they are knobcone pines, that their cones
Endure unopened on the branches, at last
To grow imbedded in the wood, waiting for fire
To open them and reseed the burned forest.
And I am waiting, alone, in the mountains,
In the forest, in the darkness, and the world
Falls swiftly on its measured ellipse.

Kenneth Rexroth

Wind Poem

Ryojirô Yamanaka

25

PART THREE

A Human Face

Drum Songs

1. The Drum-maker

He owns no car
He does not wish
to go to the capital city
make laws
drink Gordon's gin

He makes
from the living wood
in the season after rains
deep heavy drums

On the ones which are
most beautiful
he carves a human face.

Joseph Bruchac

Bums, on Waking

Bums, on waking,
Do not always find themselves
In gutters with water running over their legs
And the pillow of the curbstone
Turning hard as sleep drains from it.
Mostly, they do not know

But hope for where they shall come to.
The opening of the eye is precious,

And the shape of the body also,
Lying as it has fallen,
Disdainfully crumpling earthward
Out of alcohol.
Drunken under their eyelids
Like children sleeping toward Christmas,

They wait for the light to shine
Wherever it may decide.

Often it brings them staring
Through glass in the rich part of town,
Where the forms of humanized wax
Are arrested in midstride
With their heads turned, and dressed
By force. This is ordinary, and has come

To be disappointing.
They expect and hope for

Something totally other:
That while they staggered last night
For hours, they got clear,
Somehow, of the city; that they
Have burst through a hedge, and are lying
In a trampled rose garden,

Pillowed on a bulldog's side,
A watchdog's, whose breathing

Is like the earth's, unforced—
Or that they may, once a year
(Any dawn now), awaken
In church, not on the coffin boards
Of a back pew, or on furnace-room rags,
But on the steps of the altar

Where candles are opening their eyes
With all-seeing light

And the green stained glass of the windows
Falls on them like sanctified leaves.
Who else has quite the same
Commitment to not being sure
What he shall behold, come from sleep—
A child, a policeman, an effigy?

Who else has died and thus risen?
Never knowing how they have got there,

They might just as well have walked
On water, through walls, out of graves,
Through potter's fields and through barns,
Through slums where their stony pillows
Refused to harden, because of
Their hope for this morning's first light,

With water moving over their legs
More like living cover than it is.

                                        James Dickey

the discoveries of fire

remember
when the skin of your fingers healed
and the smoke rolled away from the
entrance to the cave   how
the rocks cooled down
and you walked back in
once animals and now
men

Lucille Clifton

Wash

For seven days it rained that June;
A storm half out to sea kept turning around like a dog
        trying to settle himself on a rug;
We were the fleas that complained in his hair.

On the eighth day, before I had risen,
My neighbors' clothes had rushed into all the back yards
And lifted up their arms in praise.

From an upstairs window it seemed prehistorical:
Through the sheds and fences and vegetable gardens,
Workshirts and nightgowns, long-soaked in the cellar,

Underpants, striped towels, diapers, child's overalls,
Bibs and black bras thronging the sunshine
With hosannas of cotton and halleluiahs of wool.

John Updike

The Term

A rumpled sheet
of brown paper
about the length

and apparent bulk
of a man was
rolling with the

wind slowly over
and over in
the street as

a car drove down
upon it and
crushed it to

the ground. Unlike
a man it rose
again rolling

with the wind over
and over to be as
it was before.

William Carlos Williams

Listening

My father could hear a little animal step,
or a moth in the dark against the screen,
and every far sound called the listening out
into places where the rest of us had never been.

More spoke to him from the soft wild night
than came to our porch for us on the wind;
we would watch him look up and his face go keen
till the walls of the world flared, widened.

My father heard so much that we still stand
inviting the quiet by turning the face,
waiting for a time when something in the night
will touch us too from that other place.

William Stafford

For a Fatherless Son

You will be aware of an absence, presently,
Growing beside you, like a tree,
A death tree, color gone, an Australian gum tree—
Balding, gelded by lightening—an illusion,
And a sky like a pig's backside, an utter lack of attention.

But right now you are dumb.
And I love your stupidity,
The blind mirror of it. I look in
And find no face but my own, and you think that's funny.
It is good for me

To have you grab my nose, a ladder rung.
One day you may touch what's wrong—
The small skulls, the smashed blue hills, the godawful hush.
Till then your smiles are found money.

Sylvia Plath

The Indians Come Down from Mixco

The Indians come down from Mixco
laden with deep blue
and the city with its frightened
streets receives them
with a handful of lights
that, like stars, are extinguished
when daybreak comes.

A sound of heartbeats
is in their hands that stroke
the wind like two oars;
and from their feet fall
prints like little soles
in the dust of the road.

The stars that peep out
at Mixco stay in Mixco
because the Indians catch them
for baskets that they fill
with chickens and the big white flowers
of the golden Spanish bayonet.

The life of the Indians
is quieter than ours,
and when they come down from Mixco
they make no sound but the panting
that sometimes hisses on their lips
like a silken serpent.

Miguel Angel Asturias
TRANSLATED BY DONALD DEVENISH WALSH

37

The Negro Speaks of Rivers

(To W. E. B. DuBois)

I've known rivers:
I've known rivers ancient as the world and older than the
      flow of human blood in human veins.

My soul has grown deep like the rivers.

I bathed in the Euphrates when dawns were young.
I built my hut near the Congo and it lulled me to sleep.
I looked upon the Nile and raised the pyramids above it.
I heard the singing of the Mississippi when Abe Lincoln
      went down to New Orleans, and I've seen its muddy
      bosom turn all golden in the sunset.

I've known rivers:
Ancient, dusky rivers.

My soul has grown deep like the rivers.

Langston Hughes

5 Ways to Kill a Man

There are many cumbersome ways to kill a man:
you can make him carry a plank of wood
to the top of a hill and nail him to it. To do this
properly you require a crowd of people
wearing sandals, a cock that crows, a cloak
to dissect, a sponge, some vinegar and one
man to hammer the nails home.

Or you can take a length of steel,
shaped and chased in a traditional way,
and attempt to pierce the metal cage he wears.
But for this you need white horses,
English trees, men with bows and arrows,
at least two flags, a prince and a
castle to hold your banquet in.

Dispensing with nobility, you may, if the wind
allows, blow gas at him. But then you need
a mile of mud sliced through with ditches,
not to mention black boots, bomb craters,
more mud, a plague of rats, a dozen songs
and some round hats made of steel.

In an age of aeroplanes, you may fly
miles above your victim and dispose of him by
pressing one small switch. All you then
require is an ocean to separate you, two
systems of government, a nation's scientists,
several factories, a psychopath and
land that no one needs for several years.

These are, as I began, cumbersome ways
to kill a man. Simpler, direct, and much more neat
is to see that he is living somewhere in the middle
of the twentieth century, and leave him there.

Edwin Brock

Kent State, May 4, 1970

Ran out of tear gas and became panicky,
poor inept kids, and therefore they poured lead
into the other kids and shot them dead,
and now myself and the whole country
are weeping. It's not a matter of degree,
not less not more than the Indo-Chinese slaughtered,
it is the same; but mostly folk are shattered
by home truths (as I know who lost my boy).

I am not willing to go on this week
with business as usual, this month this year
let cars slow down and stop and builders break
off building and close up the theater.
You see, the children that we massacre
are our own children. Call the soldiers back.

Paul Goodman

Counting Small-Boned Bodies

Let's count the bodies over again.

If we could only make the bodies smaller,
The size of skulls,
We could make a whole plain white with skulls in the
    moonlight!

If we could only make the bodies smaller,
Maybe we could get
A whole year's kill in front of us on a desk!

If we could only make the bodies smaller,
We could fit
A body into a finger-ring, for a keepsake forever.

Robert Bly

A Bummer

We were going single file
Through his rice paddies
And the farmer
Started hitting the lead track
With a rake
He wouldn't stop
The TC went to talk to him
And the farmer
Tried to hit him too
So the tracks went sideways
Side by side
Through the guy's fields
Instead of single file
Hard On, Proud Mary,
Bummer, Wallace, Rosemary's Baby
The Rutgers Road Runner
And
Go Get Em—Done Got Em
Went side by side
Through the fields
  If you have a farm in Vietnam
And a house in hell
Sell the farm
And go home

Michael Casey

track: tracked vehicle
TC: track commander

Councils

(for two voices, female and male)

♀
We must sit down
and reason together.
We must sit down.
Men standing want to hold forth.
They rain down upon faces lifted.

♂
We must sit down on the floor
on the earth
on stones and mats and blankets.
There must be no front to the speaking
no platform, no rostrum,
no stage or table.
We will not crane
to see who is speaking.

♀
Perhaps we should sit in the dark.
In the dark we could utter our feelings.
In the dark we could propose
and describe and suggest.
In the dark we could not see who speaks
and only the words
would say what they say.

♂
No one would speak more than twice,
no one would speak less than once.

♀ Thus saying what we feel and what we want,
what we fear for ourselves and each other
into the dark, perhaps we could begin
to begin to listen.

♂ Perhaps we should talk in groups
the size of new families,
never more than twenty.

♀ Perhaps we should start by speaking softly.
The women must learn to dare to speak.

♂ The men must bother to listen.

♀ The women must learn to say, I think this is so.

The men must learn to stop dancing solos
on the ceiling.
♂ After each speaks, she or he
will repeat a ritual phrase:

It is not I who speaks but the wind.
♀♂ Wind blows through me.
Long after me, is the wind.

Marge Piercy

PART FOUR

Leaving the Roots On

These Days

Whatever you have to say, leave
the roots on, let them
dangle

And the dirt
      just to make clear
      where they came from

Charles Olsen

The Red Wheelbarrow

so much depends
upon

a red wheel
barrow

glazed with rain
water

beside the white
chickens

William Carlos Williams

After Yesterday

After yesterday
afternoon's blue
clouds and white rain
the mockingbird
in the backyard
untied the drops from
leaves and twigs
with a long singing.

A. R. Ammons

Saying

I went out on
a rustling day
and
lectured the willow:
It nodded profoundly
and held
out many arms:
I held my
arms up and said things:
I spoke up:
I turned into and
from the wind:
I looked all around:
dusk, sunless,
starless, come:
the wind
fell and left us
in the open
still and bent.

A. R. Ammons

The Words

Wind, bird, and tree,
Water, grass, and light:
In half of what I write
Roughly or smoothly
Year by impatient year
The same six words recur.

I have as many floors
As meadows or rivers,
As much still air as wind
And as many cats in mind
As nests in the branches
To put an end to these.

Instead, I take what is:
The light beats on the stones,
And wind over water shines
Like long grass through the trees,
As I set loose, like birds
In a landscape, the old words.

David Wagoner

Is Is Like Is

Voices of birds are
voices of birds,
and leaves speak always like leaves,
and water is forever water
though it may hold me and my eyes
and let wind shape in.
The birds are now,
not tomorrow or yesterday,
not in anybody's grave singing,
but here where the sun is only sun
with all the trees making tree shadows
under the swinging shadow of one cloud,
and blue chairs on the deck
quietly being blue chairs,
though holding the forms
of people who have sat there
listening to bird voices and leaf talk
and holding in turn the sunlight
surrounding the dark room
where hearts beat
like all hearts,
like birds, leaves, and water.

Adrien Stoutenberg

Nothing Gold Can Stay

Nature's first green is gold,
Her hardest hue to hold.
Her early leaf's a flower;
But only so an hour.
Then leaf subsides to leaf.
So Eden sank to grief,
So dawn goes down to day.
Nothing gold can stay.

Robert Frost

Driving to Town Late to Mail a Letter

It is a cold and snowy night. The main street is deserted.
The only things moving are swirls of snow.
As I lift the mailbox door, I feel its cold iron.
There is a privacy I love in this snowy night.
Driving around, I will waste more time.

Robert Bly

PART FIVE

All Things Innocent

The Meadow Mouse

1

In a shoe box stuffed in an old nylon stocking
Sleeps the baby mouse I found in the meadow,
Where he trembled and shook beneath a stick
Till I caught him up by the tail and brought him in,
Cradled in my hand,
A little quaker, the whole body of him trembling,
His absurd whiskers sticking out like a cartoon-mouse,
His feet like small leaves,
Little lizard-feet,
Whitish and spread wide when he tried to struggle away,
Wriggling like a miniscule puppy.

Now he's eaten his three kinds of cheese and drunk from his
        bottle-cap watering-trough—
So much he just lies in one corner,
His tail curled under him, his belly big
As his head; his bat-like ears
Twitching, tilting toward the least sound.

Do I imagine he no longer trembles
When I come close to him?
He seems no longer to tremble.

2

But this morning the shoe-box house on the back porch is
    empty.
Where has he gone, my meadow-mouse,
My thumb of a child that nuzzled in my palm?—
To run under the hawk's wing,
Under the eye of the great owl watching from the elm-tree,
To live by courtesy of the shrike, the snake, the tom-cat.

I think of the nestling fallen into the deep grass,
The turtle gasping in the dusty rubble of the highway,
The paralytic stunned in the tub, and the water rising—
All things innocent, hapless, forsaken.

Theodore Roethke

Affinities

Dusk is in the cat.
It stores its shadow
in the black loft of his bones
where his ribs hang
from the spine rod.

Thunder's loose guitar
is in him,
in miniature,
and the thistle's fire.
The world is sharper
for the shape of his ears
and the blue wishbones of sparrows.

Adrien Stoutenberg

Bats

A bat is born
Naked and blind and pale.
His mother makes a pocket of her tail
And catches him. He clings to her long fur
By his thumbs and toes and teeth.
And then the mother dances through the night
Doubling and looping, soaring, somersaulting—
Her baby hangs on underneath.
All night, in happiness, she hunts and flies.
Her high sharp cries
Like shining needlepoints of sound
Go out into the night, and echoing back,
Tell her what they have touched.
She hears how far it is, how big it is,
Which way it's going:
She lives by hearing.
The mother eats the moths and gnats she catches
In full flight; in full flight
The mother drinks the water of the pond
She skims across. Her baby hangs on tight.
Her baby drinks the milk she makes him
In moonlight or starlight, in mid-air.

Their single shadow, printed on the moon
Or fluttering across the stars,
Whirls on all night; at daybreak
The tired mother flaps home to her rafter.
The others all are there.
They hang themselves up by their toes,
They wrap themselves in their brown wings.
Bunched upside-down, they sleep in air.
Their sharp ears, their sharp teeth, their quick sharp faces
Are dull and slow and mild.
All the bright day, as the mother sleeps,
She folds her wings about her sleeping child.

Randall Jarrell

Firefly

Like lamps between the trees
last evening on the road
fireflies glittered and went out

Once in a night train passing
a nameless station in a gorge
I saw similar lights flow by

To clinch the matter
this morning on the same road
I came across a firefly on a grass-blade
wearing a red hat
like a stationmaster

Kamimura Hajime
TRANSLATED BY HARRY AND LYNN GUEST
AND KAJIMA SHOZO

First Sight

Lambs that learn to walk in snow
When their bleating clouds the air
Meet a vast unwelcome, know
Nothing but a sunless glare.
Newly stumbling to and fro
All they find, outside the fold,
Is a wretched width of cold.

As they wait beside the ewe,
Her fleeces wetly caked, there lies
Hidden round them, waiting too,
Earth's immeasurable surprise.
They could not grasp it if they knew,
What so soon will wake and grow
Utterly unlike the snow.

Philip Larkin

The Bird of Night

A shadow is floating through the moonlight.
Its wings don't make a sound.
Its claws are long, its beak is bright.
Its eyes try all the corners of the night.

It calls and calls: all the air swells and heaves
And washes up and down like water.
The ear that listens to the owl believes
In death. The bat beneath the eaves,

The mouse beside the stone are still as death.
The owl's air washes them like water.
The owl goes back and forth inside the night,
And the night holds its breath.

Randall Jarrell

Bullfrog

With their lithe long strong legs
Some frogs are able
To thump upon double-
Bass strings though pond-water deadens and clogs.

But you, bullfrog, you pump out
Whole fogs full of horn—a threat
As of a liner looming. True
That, first hearing you
Disgorging your gouts of darkness like a wounded god,
Not utterly fantastical I expected
(As in some antique tale depicted)
A broken-down bull up to its belly in mud,
Sucking black swamp up, belching out black clouds

And a squall of gudgeon and lillies.
                              A surprise,

To see you, a boy's prize,
No bigger than a rat—all dumb silence
In your little old woman hands.

Ted Hughes

The Presence

Something went crabwise
across the snow this morning.
Something went hard and slow
over our hayfield.
It could have been a raccoon
lugging a knapsack,
it could have been a porcupine
carrying a tennis racket,
it could have been something
supple as a red fox
dragging the squawk and spatter
of a crippled woodcock.
Ten knuckles underground
those bones are seeds now
pure as baby teeth
lined up in the burrow.

I cross on snowshoes
cunningly woven from
the skin and sinews of
something else that went before.

Maxine Kumin

Maybe the Birds

Maybe the birds are worried
by the wind

they scream like people
in the hallway

wandering among the walls

June Jordan

Deer Among Cattle

Here and there in the searing beam
Of my hand going through the night meadow
They are all grazing

With pins of human light in their eyes.
A wild one also is eating
The human grass,

Slender, graceful, domesticated
By darkness, among the bred-
for-slaughter,

Having bounded their paralyzed fence
And inclined his branched forehead onto
Their green frosted table,
The only live thing in this flashlight
Who can leave whenever he wishes,
Turn grass into forest,

Foreclose inhuman brightness from his eyes
But stands here still, unperturbed,
In their wide-open country,

The sparks from my hand in his pupils
Unmatched anywhere among cattle,

Grazing with them the night of the hammer
As one of their own who shall rise.

James Dickey

Donkey

Sometimes he brays
Rolls in the dust
Sometimes
Then you notice him

Otherwise
You see only his ears
On the head of the planet
But he's not there

Vasko Popa
TRANSLATED BY ANNE PENNINGTON

Traveling Through the Dark

Traveling through the dark I found a deer
dead on the edge of the Wilson River road.
It is usually best to roll them into the canyon:
that road is narrow; to swerve might make more dead.

By the glow of the tail-light I stumbled back of the car
and stood by the heap, a doe, a recent killing;
she had stiffened already, almost cold.
I dragged her off: she was large in the belly.

My fingers touching her side brought me the reason—
her side was warm; her fawn lay there waiting,
alive, still, never to be born.
Beside that mountain road I hesitated.

The car aimed ahead its lowered parking lights;
Under the hood purred the steady engine.
I stood in the glare of the warm exhaust turning red;
around our group I could hear the wilderness listen.

I thought hard for us all—my only swerving—,
then pushed her over the edge into the river.

William Stafford

For a Coming Extinction

Gray whale
Now that we are sending you to The End
That great god
Tell him
That we who follow you invented forgiveness
And forgive nothing

I write as though you could understand
And I could say it
One must always pretend something
Among the dying
When you have left the seas nodding on their stalks
Empty of you
Tell him that we were made
On another day

The bewilderment will diminish like an echo
Winding along your inner mountains
Unheard by us
And find its way out
Leaving behind it the future
Dead
And ours

When you will not see again
The whale calves trying the light
Consider what you will find in the black garden
And its court
The sea cows the Great Auks the gorillas
The irreplaceable hosts ranged countless
And fore-ordaining as stars
Our sacrifices

Join your word to theirs
Tell him
That it is we who are important

W. S. Merwin

PART SIX

Is That How It Is with Poetry?

Motionless Swaying

As she jumped up to open the door,
she dropped the basket with the spools of thread—
they scattered under the table, under the chairs,
in improbable corners—one that was orange-red
got inside the lamp glass; a mauve one
deep in the mirror; that gold one—
she never had a spool of gold thread—where did it come from?
She was about to kneel, to pick them up one by one, to tidy up
before opening the door. She had no time. They knocked
   again.
She stood motionless, helpless, her hands dropped to her sides.
When she remembered to open—no one was there.

Is that how it is with poetry, then? Is this exactly how it is
   with poetry?

Yannis Ritsos
TRANSLATED BY NIKOS STANGOS

Three Riddles

Whose

Whose is that face?
At a wind's finger
it is broken and adrift

It is my face

It is my face I jump into
and fall through
I open my eyes
in a sleep of green
The horizon is over my head

till my crown bursts through
and my face takes in
as for the first time
the sky the poplars and the bright air

(puod ɐ)

Garden

The garden is framed
and hangs on the wall

It is a greenhouse
you are looking into

If you stretch out your hand
you can touch nothing
you see

But walk through
and the extent of your vision
is bounded only
by the strength of your legs

(a window)

When

When I'm on your lawn
you all go quiet
hoping to catch me

I am listening
though still

When you get too close
I take off
stretching myself out
to twice my length

Don't follow or
if you do

prepare to shrink
and tumble to strange dark

Brian Swann

(a rabbit)

Thirteen Ways of Looking at a Blackbird

I

Among twenty snowy mountains
The only moving thing
Was the eye of the blackbird.

II

I was of three minds,
Like a tree
In which there are three blackbirds.

III

The blackbird whirled in autumn winds.
It was a small part of the pantomime.

IV

A man and a woman
Are one.
A man and a woman and a blackbird
Are one.

V

I do not know which to prefer,
The beauty of inflections
Or the beauty of innuendoes,
The blackbird whistling
Or just after.

VI

Icicles filled the long window
With barbaric glass.
The shadow of the blackbird
Crossed it, to and fro.
The mood
Traced in the shadow
An undecipherable cause.

VII

O thin men of Haddam,
Why do you imagine golden birds?
Do you not see how the blackbird
Walks around the feet
Of the women about you?

VIII

I know noble accents
And lucid, inescapable rhythms;
But I know, too,
That the blackbird is involved
In what I know.

IX

When the blackbird flew out of sight,
It marked the edge
Of one of many circles.

X

At the sight of blackbirds
Flying in a green light,
Even the bawds of euphony
Would cry out sharply.

XI

He rode over Connecticut
In a glass coach.
Once, a fear pierced him,
In that he mistook
The shadow of his equipage
For blackbirds.

XII

The river is moving.
The blackbird must be flying.

XIII

It was evening all afternoon.
It was snowing
And it was going to snow.
The blackbird sat
In the cedar-limbs.

Wallace Stevens

from A Riddle

(for Ponge)

It is always handled
with a certain

caution. After all,
it is present

on so many private
occasions. It goes

into all our darkest
corners. It accepts

a continual
diminution of itself

in the act
of moving, receiving

only a touch
in return. If a girl

lays it along
her cheek, it eases

the conscience. It salves
the raw wound

nipping it clean. To be
so mobile

and miss nothing
it has to be

soft. It is.

George Macbeth

(deos)

Ripeness

You wake up feeling
like an oven
where bread
has just been baked.

All night the yeast rose
and at dawn
you baked the bread,
a round full loaf.

Ruth Whitman

Dawn

Quick cold hands
One by one remove
The bandages from the darkness
I open my eyes
         I am alive
Still
       in the middle
Of a wound still fresh.

Octavio Paz

Storm End

Sudden and from horizon to horizon driven steady
a scythe of light

It has not leveled has raised up
between the four horizons
every
rock
tree
slope
corrie
grass
ferncrystal

harvest as far as sight
standing.

Jonathan Griffin

PART SEVEN

A Place for the Genuine

Poetry

I, too, dislike it: there are things that are important beyond
 all this fiddle.
Reading it, however, with a perfect contempt for it, one dis-
 covers that there is in
it after all, a place for the genuine.
 Hands that can grasp, eyes
 that can dilate, hair that can rise
 if it must, these things are important not because a

high sounding interpretation can be put upon them but
 because they are
useful; when they become so derivative as to become unin-
 telligible,
the same thing may be said for all of us, that we
 do not admire what
 we cannot understand: the bat,
 holding on upside down or in quest of something to

eat, elephants pushing, a wild horse taking a roll, a tireless
 wolf under
a tree, the immovable critic, twitching his skin like a horse
 that fells a flea, the base-
 ball fan, the statistician—
 nor is it valid
 to discriminate against "business documents and

school books"; all these phenomena are important. One must
		make a distinction
however: when dragged into prominence by half poets, the
		result is not poetry,
nor till the poets among us can be
		"literalists of
			the imagination"—above
			insolence and triviality and can present

for inspection, imaginary gardens with real toads in them,
		shall we have
it. In the meantime, if you demand on one hand,
the raw material of poetry in
all its rawness and
that which is on the other hand
genuine, then you are interested in poetry.

Marianne Moore

XIV

I don't bother with rhymes. It is seldom
That there are two trees equal, side by side.
I think and write as the flowers have colour
But with less perfection in my way of expressing myself
Because I lack the divine simplicity
Of being all only my outside.

I look and am moved.
I am moved as water flows when the ground is sloping,
And my poetry is natural like the rising of a wind . . .

Alberto Caeiro
(Fernando Pessoa)
TRANSLATED BY JONATHAN GRIFFIN

from Manifesto

Ladies and gentlemen
This is our final word
—Our first and final word—
The poets have come down from Olympus.

For the old folks
Poetry was a luxury item
But for us
It's an absolute necessity
We couldn't live without poetry.

Unlike our elders
—And I say this with all respect—
We maintain this
A poet is no alchemist
A poet is a man like all men
A bricklayer building his wall:
A maker of windows and doors.

We talk
with everyday words
We don't believe in cabalistic signs.

And one thing more:
The poet is there
To see to it the tree does not grow crooked.

Nicanor Parra
TRANSLATED BY MILLER WILLIAMS

Section Notes

I. *The Muscle in Your Heart*

YOUNG SOUL by Imamu Amiri Baraka:
Baraka wrote his early works under the name of Leroi
Jones.

II. *How Deep the Earth Can Be*

SONG OF THE SKY LOOM by the Tewa Indians:
This is one of the tribal chants of the Tewa, pueblo-
dwelling Indians from the Rio Grande Valley of New
Mexico and Arizona. They were, like their Navajo
neighbors, skilled weavers.

AFTER THE RAIN by Yannis Ritsos:
Yannis Ritsos (b. 1909) is a major Greek poet.
Throughout his life he has been an outspoken critic of
fascism, and has been imprisoned for his views. Dur-
ing the dictatorship of Metaxas, in the 1930s, Ritsos'
books were burned.

INVISIBLE PRINTS by Tamura Ryuichi:
Tamura Ryuichi (b. 1923) is considered to be Japan's
best-known contemporary poet.

INVERSELY, AS THE SQUARE OF THEIR DIS-
TANCES APART by Kenneth Rexroth:
The title refers to the equation, in physics, which de-
scribes the attraction of two bodies.

WIND by Yamanaka Ryojiro:
Yamanaka Ryojiro (b. 1920) comes from northern Ja-

pan. His work has its English equivalent in "concrete poetry" which uses words, and sometimes sounds, to form a "concrete" image, or configuration on the page. Yamanaka is a painter and typographer as well as a poet.

III. *A Human Face*

THE INDIANS COME DOWN FROM MIXCO by Miguel Angel Asturias:
Miguel Angel Asturias (b. 1899) is a Guatemalan poet, novelist, and diplomat who won the Nobel Prize for Literature in 1967. His studies of Indian folklore have deeply influenced his poetry.

KENT STATE by Paul Goodman:
On May 4, 1970, four students were killed and nine others wounded by National Guardsmen during an antiwar demonstration at Kent State College, in Ohio.

V. *All Things Innocent*

FIREFLY by Kamimura Hajime:
Kamimura Hajime (b. 1910) comes from Nagasaki and runs a secondhand bookshop in Kyushu.

DONKEY by Vasko Popa:
Vasko Popa (b. 1922) is one of the leading poets of Yugoslavia. He has published four volumes of poetry, and his poetic vision, shaped by the war and postwar chaos of Eastern Europe, is, according to Ted Hughes, "among the purest, most wide awake of living poets."

VI. *Is That How It Is With Poetry?*

DAWN by Octavio Paz:
Octavio Paz (b. 1914) is one of Mexico's best-known

living writers, and a major poet of the Spanish language. He fought for the Republic during the Spanish Civil War, and later served his own country as a diplomat. His last post was Ambassador to India. Paz has published ten books of poetry and many landmark essays on culture, language, and ethnology.

VII. *A Place for the Genuine*

XIV by Alberto Caiero (Fernando Pessoa):
Alberto Caiero is one of the three pseudonyms of Fernando Pessoa (1888–1935). Pessoa, Portugal's greatest modern poet, wrote four bodies of work, one under his own name, and one as Alberto Caiero, Ricardo Reis, and Alvaro da Campos, respectively. Each has a vividly distinct style, subject matter, and personal philosophy. Caiero was a nature poet.

THE POETS COME DOWN FROM OLYMPUS by Nicanor Parra:
Nicanor Parra is a Chilean poet who has received his country's National Literature Prize. His poems, which he calls "anti-poems," challenge the aesthetic—and political—status quo.

Index

99

74997

Centralia Junior High School
Centralia, Washington